NEVER SAY CAN'T!

NEVER SAY CAN'T!

Chrys Phillips

iUniverse®

NEVER SAY CAN'T!

Images envato
Graphics Mikaela Phillips

iUniverse books may be ordered through booksellers or by contacting:

iUniverse
1663 Liberty Drive
Bloomington, IN 47403
www.iuniverse.com
1-800-Authors (1-800-288-4677)

ISBN: 978-1-4917-7161-7 (sc)
ISBN: 978-1-4917-7162-4 (hc)
ISBN: 978-1-4917-7163-1 (e)

Library of Congress Control Number: 2015911361

Print information available on the last page.

iUniverse rev. date: 09/18/2015

For my Mikaela
And for you!

NOTE FROM
THE AUTHOR ...

Imagine living in a world where you feel totally empowered!

That you never feel the burdens of stress, fear, anxiety, worry or any type of concerns ... the only emotions you can feel is happiness and contentment. A true sense of security within yourself, now wouldn't that be bliss?

I guess if it was that easy we all would be feeling these emotions every day. However, it seems in our daily life there's always someone or something that seems to change or alter that feeling of bliss and thus, it overpowers our emotions. Then, we sometimes begin to feel sad or negative and our inner empowerment starts to wane.

Empowerment, is such a powerful word. *EMPOWERMENT!* The ability for you to feel total inner strength and be yourself.

This is your mission in your life's journey for without it, it's a roller coaster of many consuming emotions and losses that you don't always need. Basically, life's a rollercoaster ride anyway, and without the excess baggage it's much easier.

First and foremost there's no miracle formula and there is no secret potion or method to have inner empowerment. However, there is one step to always moving towards having that inner feeling and that's learning how ... *to believe in you*! To believe when the world says no to you that only you can define who you are and only you can define where you go in life!

NEVER ALLOW ANYONE TO DEFINE WHO YOU ARE!

When I wrote the first manuscript of this book over four years ago, it was to basically share my outlook and my life experiences of how I kept myself empowered throughout my life. My life was no bed of roses. My childhood consisted of living with many families and also there were times when I was on my own renting, and I couldn't afford food.

When I experienced true set backs and hurdles I kept myself going forward and tried not to look back or focus on my difficult situation in that particular moment. Sure I had many bad days that I felt too low to even care, but somehow I dug deep again and found inner strength to decide that no one or nothing was going to keep putting me down! That I was going to break out of the cycle and be free, be successful and be in control, as much as I could possibly achieve in my life.

This book isn't to narrate a step by step autobiography of the many hardships I went through it's to focus on the essence, that if I can get through it even when I was being knocked down, emotionally, physically and spiritually again and again, that you can too!

I believe it's a journey to read this book that I've written in an easy format allowing not to overload the reader with continuous extensive chapters. I talk about the focal fundamentals in a relaxed manner. It's a journey to read and discover more about yourself and you shall always then have an understanding to say when it seems impossible ... NEVER SAY CAN'T! I CAN!

In my journey, I've known days of having no home to go to, to never experiencing nurturing from parents or any emotional support, or even a basic hug growing up. I was always hiding my true home life. I had friends who didn't really know what I was going through. I was studious and also very friendly, there was no obvious chip on my shoulder of burdens or sadness. I just kept moving forward. Many of my dreams when growing up no matter what I did or tried, I lost them. Sometimes it was due to having no money and opportunities were lost and some dreams/goals vanished one after another. It was horrible and it was sometimes hard to watch others with families have the opportunity to do whatever they wanted socially and with their education. However I did not want to fail and I decided to alter my dream, to find another road for that dream and I always kept re-inventing my path towards my dream, to ensure it did not vanish! The dream over the years did change from a teenager to being an adult, BUT the essence never varied. The essence was freedom with success. To live a life that everyone told me I would never have, as I came from nothing. The idea of the dream may have had to change but the essence didn't and the ability to re-invent my dream to achieve its goal was always grounded within me!

Therefore, your dreams may not always be in your destiny in that particular desired moment, but it is up to you whether you go to pieces and allow it to consume you in a defeated manner and be a victim to that outcome. Or do you decide to stay strong and believe in yourself that you can be part of another dream that you begin creating! There's no shame or defeat in changing your dreams or goals even if it happens time again and again, the real shame would be in not creating a new dream for yourself or following another path with the same dream. Either way, if you get kicked down just decide not to stay down!

I feel inspired and pleased that you found this book and may it bring you the assistance on your journey to arriving to your infinite dreams …

Chrys xoxo

Never allow anyone to define you!

EMPOWERMENT

(n.) The process of becoming
stronger and more confident

The biggest questions people have are, how can I become empowered in my life …

- When I don't have enough money?
- If I don't really know what I want to do?
- If I've tried before and it didn't work?
- If every time I try to do something, something stops me?
- If I don't know who to talk to about it?
- If I'm not sure I can really do what I dream of?
- If I'm not good enough?
- If I'm not smart enough?
- If it's easier for others who have more than what I have?

This is only some of the questions that people have when trying to achieve a goal or a dream, which in turn begins your self-empowerment. These types of questions that everyone experiences ultimately can become the obstacle that stops you from moving forward. That's why, throughout this book we will cover some brief exercises and easy techniques, to build a basic foundation to allow you to understand more of what you require to achieve your dreams and goals that shall lead to your self-empowerment. This allows you skills to always reflect back on.

Without having questions like these, you wouldn't be able to source the solutions to move forward in obtaining what you desire. Your goal or your dreams can be many. They can include an array of choices, from a grade you want in your education, or traveling, or even beginning the road to your dream job and/or your own business. No matter how simple or complex your ultimate goal is, you can only reach it by knowing how to be self-empowered. The definition of the word empowerment tells us that it's *a process of becoming stronger and more confident* therefore, you can begin today on any goal you have and therefore you have begun the process of reaching your own empowerment and learning a vital skill in succeeding!

It's easy for you to write down every dream you have and say this is what I want. The tricky part is to keep your self-belief true. Some of you shall have people that shall respect your dreams and support you, whereas others may experience the negativity of being told that you cannot achieve this or do this. You must remember even if the world is telling you, you can't or even if there is no one saying that you can, it's up to you to decide that you can follow your dreams/goals!

As I mentioned in the beginning of the book, in my, *Notes from the Author*, you have to remember, to never allow anyone to define who you are! Otherwise you shall never reach what you want, you will be living the life they want you to live.

Just for a moment, we can view the questions listed above. Most of these questions are basically saying *I don't have enough faith in myself to do what I want or find the answers to assist myself to achieve what I want.* There's nothing wrong with that, it's just our brain and our emotions telling us concerns we have but, if these concerns become the only factors you concentrate on, then you won't be able to empower yourself to succeed because you have already put a limitation on yourself. What you need to do, is to eliminate any types of questions and begin writing down and planning what it is you want to achieve. It's time to start asking the correct questions to begin your self-empowered journey!

Take a moment to fill in these graphs. Write down your likes, dislikes, hobbies and interests. Use a pencil as then you can always refresh your answers and goals.

Who am I?

LIKES	DISLIKES

HOBBIES	INTERESTS

My Dreams/Goals

SHORT TERM

_____

_____

_____

_____

_____

LONG TERM

_____

_____

_____

_____

_____

With these graphs you've answered, inclusive of:

- Likes & Dislikes
- Hobbies & Interests
- Short term & Long term goals/dreams

You now have the beginning of a basic blueprint of who you are. These questions obviously change over time and that's okay, because as you evolve, your interests and goals shall change with you. The key here is, to keep sight of what your ultimate goal is and in this moment, it is self-empowerment.

Self-empowerment does not mean being self-absorbed or acting from your ego. In fact, it's the opposite. Self-empowerment is knowing and believing that you have what it takes to handle whatever comes your way and therefore being able to act in a manner that supports your ultimate goals.

INFLUENCES

(v.) having the power to
produce effects on ones actions,
behavior and opinions

Everybody has positive and negative influences in their daily routines. Sadly sometimes it's the people you most cherish that can have a negative influence on you. People that you cherish can also have a positive reinforcement and influence you in your daily life. Your definition of yourself should come from you, not anyone else, love who you are as you are.

Inevitably some people will be a negative influence just because they think they can. Whether it's a bully, or someone with limited vision, or just someone who just seems to focus on negativity, it's how it is; therefore in many various situations you may encounter this and no matter how hard it is, as it isn't always easy to ignore someone's behavior or interaction with you. You must be strong within yourself, believe you have the power to choose whether you allow their opinion to dictate who you are.

When you have a personal goal, no matter what it is, this goal of the achievement is what acts as a catalyst to keep you focused on your journey and not be focused on other peoples *influences* of what they think you are worth. Your goals and dreams are your catalyst to feel inner strength and belief in your self-empowerment. Keep going!

In contrast to this, some people are a positive influence in your life. These are the people that you want surrounding you. This could be a mentor, friend, family member, or even a person that you don't know but they are your role model.

It is not easy to ignore people who are hurtful, however how you react continuously to these experiences shall ultimately define who you become. If you believe in yourself, even if nobody else does, then you are already shutting out negative influences. There's no quick fix that can keep you having self-belief to achieve your own empowerment, it's an exercise that you focus on daily, just like any other type of training or studies to achieve knowledge and success. You have to decide when you are in the pathway of various influences, *Am I going to be a victim to this negative situation? Or am I going to be my own hero?*

Now that you've previously written down various points about yourself, you can begin to decide, what are the goals you want to begin with? Short term goals are obviously the ones you begin with however, you can still be working towards your long term goals too.

This next diagram depicts you in the middle with the influences surrounding you. This is a basic outline of what influences us, as everyone is an individual and some people don't have much family or many friends, but you can view this diagram to understand and think about who does influence you everyday and personalize it to suit you.

Who inspires you? Famous or not

Who does or doesn't understand you?

FAMILY

WANTS   **ME**   FEARS

FRIENDS

This diagram is to simply show you a few basic daily influences. That being said, of course there are many other factors that are based on your notes from the previous chapter, *Empowerment.* First and foremost, your likes and dislikes influence you. They make up your disposition and what your passions are too.

However, this diagram is not to encompass your inner influences, this chapter is to discuss, your external influences and their impact on your inner feelings.

Family and friends consists of who ever you want to call your family and friends. In this day and age, families can consist of close friends too. Therefore when glancing at this diagram you need to consider who the supportive people are in your life and who are the disapproving people in your life.

Why do you need to do this? The simplest answer to this is, that you need to have a clear knowledge of who uplifts you and who brings you down. To achieve self empowerment you have to know where you stand with people to ensure you are protecting your inner-self, to allow no one or anything to define you or limit you.

Each one of us is an individual and that's what makes you, *you!*

Whether or not you feel different, whether or not you want to do something different, it's your journey. Whether or not you're in a clique or have no family or close friends its not relevant to what defines you. What you are is unique and that's your own blueprint. And outside influences or situations do not ultimately define you. Clearly believe and know only you have the power to define you!

It shouldn't matter what ethnicity, what gender, or what appearance you have, what ultimately makes you is being true to yourself.

The bottom line is … NEVER ALLOW ANYONE TO DEFINE YOU!

Take a glance once again at this exercise and then write down your thoughts. This exercise shall shed light on what and who these categories consist of. Knowing your fears and your wants, is a powerful tool. If you know what your fear is, then you already know what's limiting you and how you can begin to overcome it. Once you desire your wants/goals with true dedication and passion it will ultimately out way your fears. Fears are usually misplaced limitations, placed on yourself possibly through influences around you or previous experiences. However, if you start to delve within yourself with these questions, you shall be able to face some of your fears and move forward with drive and enthusiasm to achieve your goals. If you ever feel totally overwhelmed always remember you can talk to a professional counselor, doctor or coach to assist you in settling and solving the overwhelming fears or questions you may have.

POSITIVE INFLUENCES

_____

_____

_____

_____

_____

_____

NEGATIVE INFLUENCES

_____

_____

_____

_____

_____

_____

FAMILY	FRIENDS
WANTS	**FEARS**

FOCUS

(v.) to concentrate and be diligent

Without having a clear focus on your goals and staying true to yourself, you won't achieve what you started out wanting to create.

People make the mistake of thinking, *yeah, I really want this and I'm going to get it.* Just by saying it and writing it down or even talking about it, it doesn't mean anything shall be achieved without constant diligence in knuckling down and beginning what you said you want to achieve.

It doesn't matter how old you are, taking the first steps to achieve anything is better than allowing time and opportunity to pass you by and then watching somebody else achieve what you wanted. Over the years I have never given up. I had no financial network or supportive family network, but I decided that, that was not going to define who I wanted to be.

You are only limited in your journey as much as you believe you are.

Keeping a *focus* on your goals should be a daily, weekly, monthly experience. Without *focus* nothing ever gets done, because if you're not deciding where your journey is going, somebody else is going to decide that for you.

TIPS TO STAY FOCUSED

- Read my quotes chapter and then:

    ❖ Write down some of these quotes on notes for yourself and place them in your room, your desk, diary etc.
    ❖ Stick post-its of your favorite quotes for easy access to read them
    ❖ Refer to the quotes chapter, when you feel down and keep focused

- Create a folder or journal that organizes your tasks towards your goals/dreams

- Devise a current To-Do list, that you can look over to assess what you have achieved and still need to achieve towards your goals

- Manage your time. With everything else going on in your life, ensure to make 'you time' that allows you to stay fresh, focused and enthusiastic about your journey

- When you experience negative influences, focus on your goals as this can help ignore the negativity, because you are focused on your strengths and what you are achieving

- Staying focused… it's truly up to you. You cannot achieve, if you believe you can't!

Remember: NEVER SAY CAN'T!

DREAM IT!
BELIEVE IT!
ENVISION IT!
STRIVE FOR IT!
FOCUS ON IT!
AND GO FOR IT!

REVIEW

(v.) evaluating (something) with the possibility or intention of evolving change if necessary

What happens when it goes wrong?

The interesting and important part of achieving your goals is to constantly review your journey and any crossroads you may come across. Look over your notes, look over your time frame and consider the following:

- What have I achieved?
- How do I feel more empowered?
- I didn't allow that persons negativity to hurt me
- I feel pleased with what I'm doing
- I'm focused
- What's my next step?
- I'm not afraid of failing now that I've experienced some success

There are millions of questions you can ask yourself here that would be diversely different for each one of us. However, the generic consensus of anyone's goals is how are you feeling about it and what have you achieved thus far? Write down a weekly evaluation or a monthly evaluation of what you are achieving personally and achieving towards your goals. This enables you to see that you are probably achieving more than you thought and it also allows you to evaluate what needs to be done, as you evolve on your journey. Don't forget to always evaluate and re-invent your goals to ultimately achieve self-empowerment through believing in yourself and following what your sporting, creative, intellectual, hobbies and educational/career goals are for you.

Call To Action!

You've been diligently working towards your goals and out of nowhere something comes up that stops you. This is where you have to review your particular goal that has hit a hurdle. Is the factor and the hurdle that you've come across something that you can change?

Or is it something that you have no control over? Either way, the most important factor to remember is this, no matter what comes your way, you have to find a way to go around the hurdle, whether that be extending your goal time frame or re-inventing your goal.

What does this really mean?

This means depending on your situation, you do not have to surrender defeat, you have to consider re-inventing your goal. That could be, swapping the path you've chosen to achieve it and finding another option for it. Sometimes these hurdles are hidden opportunities for you to re-evaluate what is the core essence of what you want to achieve. By keeping the desired fundamentals of where you personally want to be in your journey to achieve success, then you can always re-invent and review the situation and goal surrounding you by reviewing a new plan.

Keep your focus on the *true meaning* of the goal, not always the static image of what it has to be. For example, you may be creative but cannot afford to do a career/education you desire but your passion to be successful in the arts can be re-invented to another creative field.

For example, you want to be a leading fashion journalist for a high-end publication but you have personal commitments and you cannot relocate/move to where the job/education requires you. Once you allow yourself to feel this disappointment, you have to turn that disappointment into *I still want to be a success in the fashion industry, what do I do?*

Learn everything there is to know about blogging and start a great fashion blog

Possibly, submit freelance editorials to various fashion publications

Try to find equivalent courses to study part time, while working in the fashion industry

Look at other careers within fashion such as: photography, merchandising, fashion consultant …

For example, you want to play in the NFL but an injury won't allow it, once you allow yourself to feel this disappointment, you have to turn this disappointment into *I still want to be a success in the sporting industry, what do I do?*
Possibly, try another sport, that doesn't hinder your injury or
Think of becoming a trainer/coach
Think of sports management …

Even though these examples are generic, the point here is to learn that your goals/dreams have to consist of an essence, not a tangible fix and that is why it is paramount to always *review* your goals and have the ability to reinvent your journey if required.

KEEP ON!
KEEP DREAMING!

Don't allow hurdles to stop you!

BE WHAT YOU SET OUT TO BECOME!

ENTREPENEUR

(n.) a person who manages
a business/idea with
considerable initiative

Have you ever thought of putting your time and interest into an idea that you are passionate about?

The reason why I added this chapter is because we are all individuals. Some of you will have a clear idea of what your focus/career shall be, however, many of you may be up and coming entrepreneurs. This is a great time to think about your ambitions and your future. Starting a business is a thriving trend for anyone fuelled with drive and the insight to be resourceful, no matter what your current lifestyle is. Here are some informative tips to consider if this is for you and how to begin being an entrepreneur with an idea/business you have thought of.

1. Begin by building a solid foundation of the fundamentals you are considering. Include a well constructed list and business profile of what your idea is. Write down and brainstorm these components. Include who your market is, what's unique about your product or service, how can you create it? Do you require assistance to create it? What resources do you need to utilize? Is there any money involved to create or promote it? Are you going to be committed to the time required to achieve success? How dedicated are you to it? Where can you promote this business/service/idea? Are there grants for you?

Once you've asked yourselves these type of questions, then you have an understanding of what it is you want to achieve. You must do some research by reading business and entrepreneurial books, also auto-biographies of successful people. This shall give you an insight into what they experienced and how it could relate to you. It also would have great information for your path in becoming an entrepreneur.

This chapter is to shed some light on the possibility that you could be an entrepreneur and to inspire that notion in you that you may never have thought about giving it a go. By no means am I saying, by reading this concise chapter, that this is the only method it takes to succeed as an entrepreneur, this chapter is to inspire you to begin that journey that you may never have considered.

NEVER SAY CAN'T!

2. Social media is a pivotal point of contact to build online relationships with perspective customers, it is also a very cost-effective method of promotion.

3. If possible, research some courses or classes to assist you.

4. You may also source a mentor, to assist you in your entrepreneur path.

5. Networking is a great way to talk about your idea and gain business contacts too

SELF LOVE

(n.) regard for one's own
well being and happiness

Self Love.

This doesn't mean to be an egomaniac and to believe that you are the ultimate at everything and that in love with yourself … ha ha! The true importance of this chapter is to love and accept yourself as you are. You don't need to seek other people's acceptance, you just need to love yourself as the unique individual that you are!

Making a commitment to yourself to believe in yourself and accept yourself, as you are! This must begin in this moment that you are reading this. It's not the easiest thing to do as there are many outside *influences* that make us question our worth. Therefore, once again the earlier chapter of *Influences* comes into play for this chapter too. It's an ongoing evolution of focusing on your self in an accepting and loving manner, even when some days it's not easy. Always refer back to chapter two and think about what's happening and if you're over judging your appearance, intelligence, beliefs, emotions and basically, whatever makes you, you! You don't need the world to accept you, you only need to accept yourself as you are.

Keep evolving and aspiring to learn new points of view, knowledge and opportunities as this too continues to nurture who you are.

Being able to commit to this ongoing, evolving belief for yourself of self acceptance, can also influence the quality of decisions you make. The more calm, accepting, happy and open-minded you are, then you can instigate decisions worthy of you. Therefore, you need to keep your self perception with a loving and nurturing approach. Think about your qualities and what you like about yourself.

MY QUALITIES	WHAT I LIKE ABOUT ME

Here are a few points to consider, to assist you in your journey of self appreciation.

1. Keep a journal.

   Having a journal where you can write down your thoughts clearly inclusive of what your thankful for each day creates an affirmative reflection

2. Meditation.

   To slow down your breathing and brain overly thinking even if it's for five minutes in your day, try to begin a meditation regime, to suit you.

3. Begin your day with a motivating or inspiring thought no matter what's going on around you. You can read the quotes in this book, open up a page in the quotes chapter and spontaneously come across a quote and read it to inspire you.

4. Activities/ Interests.

   Consider expanding your activities or even beginning a new interest. This allows you to spend more 'you' time and possibly meet new people and learn interesting skills/ hobbies.

5. Own your worth!

   Once again, this is not the easiest belief to have when many influences can affect and condition your perception. However, you have the power to define yourself!

6. Forgiving.

   Sometimes we make mistakes or have bad days, even months, or even years. This is when we have to forgive ourselves, not to be too hard on ourselves or have constant harsh judgments. You need to let go, move on and learn from whatever the situation entailed.

7. Think About It.

Imagine a life where you always believe in your worth without ego and with true empowering confidence. It would be FANTASTIC! It may not always be the simplest thing to do, but now you have the opportunity to achieve this.

8. Professional Assistance.

If you find yourself sinking into further unhealthy thoughts, moods and feelings, you could seek professional advice from a support group, doctor, coach or counselor. There's nothing wrong with investing in yourself to tap into your true worth! Don't neglect yourself if you need assistance and professional advice, as it's the next step to moving forward to where you want to be.

CONSERVATION

(n.) the action of preserving and protecting (something) in particular

Before moving onto the quotes chapter of this book, this is a brief authors note to tell you how passionate I am, about conserving our rainforests, protecting our planet and its various flora and fauna.

Therefore, you may find it just as rewarding to do something for your planet and/or humanity.

There is nothing more rewarding than when you are in a situation of being able to give back to our society and our planet.

I have many more ideas of what future foundations I want to create and assist with and to reach out to those in need. I also support the foundations listed on my webpage in whatever capacity I can. In whatever capacity you or I can assist, we can do something every day no matter what it is, it's paramount to always assist where we can!

There's many foundations, organizations and charities around the globe.

This conservation page is to allow another option you may have considered or not considered, thus moving you to volunteer or assist in any capacity and find a very rewarding experience for yourself, while helping others.

YOU HAVE THE

POWER

TO SAY TODAY,
I AM
ME!
AND BEING

ME

IS WHO
I WANT
TO
BE

Having a bad day?

DO SOMETHING THAT IS

FOCUSED

ON

YOUR

GOALS

Forget the negatives

Today's
your
chance
to
do
whatever
you
dream of!
Just begin

Step

By

Step

REMEMBER TO RELAX & DO SOMETHING FOR YOURSELF

FLY WITH YOUR...

Passions,
Dreams,
Goals, Ideas

AND LAND AS HIGH
AS YOU DARE TO
AIM

DONT WASTE TIME FEELNG SORRY FOR YOURSELF.

IT ONLY USES UP YOUR TIME

Don t allow thE ones
who tR ied to stop you
WIN

BE the person you Want to
bE!

Live it

aND

gEt what

you

deserve!

When

come your way,

ride them out

without forgetting

who

you are

You desire
your
life to change

Then get up
and
open a different door
you never
did before
and
see what you may
find

Look beyond the limitations-
people place
on you

focus on how you
can achieve your dreams

Believe in who you are
and what your worth is.

No one else should be telling
you your worth, but you!

~

Without passion for it and without drive, keep moving towards it …

~

ANYTHING DONE WITH

LOVE

and passion

BRINGS REWARDS

Cherish your

dreams

and

keep on

dreaming

REMEMBER ...

~ believe in you

~ have your dreams

~ use your imagination

~ stand true no matter what they say

~ only you can define who you are

~ make a difference

~ self empowerment comes from doing not saying

~ keep on!

~ when they knock you down, get back up

~ love what you do

~ show compassion

~ don't judge

~ just be you!

If it goes crap today,

But how are you going to react?

Don't be a victim to it!

focus on your

DREAMS

IF YOU FEEL LIKE ESCAPING WHEN

IT SEEMS TOO MUCH THEN

GO TO YOUR FAVORITE PLACE

AND JUST RELAX!

It's ok and normal to have bad days.

How

can

YOU

take

THAT

risk

TO

never

TRY?

~

When they say they love you but
walkaway from you, cry
but never lose who you
are as they never saw the
true you, to stay!

~

DON'T BE LAZY WITH YOUR DESTINY,

BEGIN SHAPING IT NOW!

It's not easy to be different when you are pushed into following

STAND

TRUE

AND

BE

YOU!

BE THE
ULTIMATE

Live your life

and remember to see

the beauty in others

With

inner
strength

comes

greatness!

Your imagination, dreams & goals are yours!
GRAB THEM!

Fear

is what you feel when
you believe you cant,

but you can choose to say

I CAN!

IGNORE THE HATERS!

*have everything within
you to be empowered!*

*Don't search for
it from others*

can do it!

you

ARE EVERYTHING YOU

NEED TO BE TO MAKE THE

Change

TO REACH YOUR

dreams

TO

Succeed!

JUST

Believe!

Live in fear and you'll have no life.

Have a

can -do

attitude!

DARE
TO
TRY !

When the people surrounding you don't understand your dreams and goals, its okay. They don't need to. Its your journey not theirs.

keep moving
towards
your
dreams
don't stop
your
journey

no

matter

how

old

you are

you

can

achieve

anything

Aim for the

highest

levels

Why settle for

lower?

Look beyond limitations people place on you

and

focus on how you can achieve

YOUR DREAMS

believe
you
can!

NEVER SAY CAN'T!

SAY HOW CAN I . . .

Printed in the United States
By Bookmasters